Blasphemy

Grace

Quarrels

&

Reconciliation

The
OBSCURE
Bible Study Series

Grow in your faith through investigating unusual biblical characters.

The OBSCURE Bible Study Series

Blasphemy, Grace, Quarrels & Reconciliation

The intriguing lives of first century disciples.

Book 2 – Personal Study Guide

Stephen H Berkey

GETWISDOM PUBLISHING

COPYRIGHT

RESOURCES

*Blessed is the one who finds wisdom, and the one
who gets understanding.* (Proverbs 3:13 ESV)

You can access free resources from Get Wisdom by going to:

www.getwisdom.link/resources

You will always find:

1   Free Sample Study Lesson: "*Shamgar*" (PDF)

2   Free Worksheets for recording answers.
     For use by those who have an ebook or do not
     want to write in their hardcopy book.

You may find:

Other free materials that will be useful in your daily life, Bible
study, or relationships.

TABLE OF CONTENTS

CONTENTS

ABOUT THE LEADER GUIDE

All of the books in this Bible Study series have an extensive Leader Guide. If you are a participant in a group, a Leader Guide is not necessary, unless you want the author's answers. If you are studying independently, you may want the Leader Guide.

In the Guide the answers follow the questions with a small amount of space for the Leader's personal responses. If you are using the Leader Guide and want to do the study without the influence of the author's answers the best solution is to obtain the blank Worksheets, which are free. This will allow you to record your answers separately before reviewing the answers in the Leader Guide.

You can access the Worksheets by going to our website and entering your email address:

www.getwisdom.link/resources

Why Study OBSCURE Characters?

Unique, New, and Fresh

For experienced Bible students these characters will provide a fresh and interesting approach to Bible study. Since most of the material will be unfamiliar to the participants, new believers or those just starting Bible study should not feel intimidated by students who have been studying for years. Most readers will not be acquainted with the majority of the characters and events in this series.

Knowledge of Scripture

These studies are a great introduction for those just beginning Bible study. Regardless of their level of knowledge, everyone should find the characters and stories provide an opportunity to grow in their faith through investigating fascinating and unusual biblical stories and incidents.

Valuable Life Lessons

These lesser-known characters are a lot like you and me. God uses all sorts of people to accomplish His plans! You will become familiar with ordinary people, strange characters, and people living on the fringe of life who have the same troubles and challenges as people today. The deep truths and life lessons embedded in these studies should be valuable. They will provide new insights to scripture.

INTRODUCTION

Description of Series

This unique series uses a number of lesser-known Bible characters and events to explore such major themes as Angels, being Born Again, Courage, Death, Evangelism, Faithfulness, Forgiveness, Grace, Hell, Leadership, Miracles, the Remnant, the Sabbath, Salvation, Rebellion, Sovereignty, Thankfulness, Women, the World, Creation, and End Times.

The series as a whole provides both a broad and fresh understanding of the nature of God as we see Him act in the lives of people we've never examined before.

Most of the people chosen for these studies are unfamiliar because they are mentioned only a few times in Scripture – fifteen only once or twice. Others, although more familiar, are included because of their particular contribution to kingdom work.

For example, Scripture mentions Shamgar only twice. One verse in Judges 3:31 tells his story and 5:6 simply establishes a timeline and says nothing more about him. Then there is Nicodemus, with whom we associate the concept of being "born again." His name appears only 5 times, all in one short passage in the book of John. Eve, although obviously not obscure, is included in order to investigate the creation story.

Book Description

Book 9 in the OBSCURE series is about the person Jesus Christ. We examine a number of characters closely associated with Jesus. The first is the priest Melchizedek. The primary focus of this lesson is on the superiority of Christ and the argument outlined in the book of Hebrews on that subject. We then examine one of the many scribes identified in the Bible. This is the scribe who said "I will follow you wherever you go," but Jesus questioned his priorities and his commitment.

Nicodemus is an interesting character because he was a Pharisee and he came at night seeking answers from Jesus. Jesus told Nicodemus that he had to be born again, but Nicodemus had difficulty understanding what Jesus was talking about.

Lazarus is the only character in any of the Biblical parables who is identified by name. He and a rich man had died and Lazarus was carried by the angels to Abraham's side. The rich man was in Hades. This story allows us to take an in-depth look at the subject of hell.

As we near the crucifixion the next lesson is Jesus on the cross with a criminal who knew who Jesus was and said, "Jesus, remember me when you come into your kingdom." Then Jesus made a remarkable promise: "Today you will be with me in Paradise."

Following the crucifixion Jesus appeared to two disciples walking home to Emmaus from Jerusalem. They had lost all hope and were deeply saddened by the events that had just taken place. Then Jesus joined them on the road, but they were kept from recognizing Him until he broke bread at the evening meal and blessed it.

The next subject is a gospel conversation, and we find Philip running down a dusty road to talk with an Ethiopian eunuch who had been in Jerusalem. Philip opened the conversation by asking, "How can I help?" and the result was that the eunuch later asked to be baptized.

Lastly, we look at the story in Acts describing Jason who hosted Paul and Silas in Thessalonica. Paul was being pursued and persecuted by the Jews and when they could not find Paul they took their anger out on Jason. This allows us to closely examine the subject of the Messiah.

Group Discussion or Individual Study

These studies can be done individually or in a small discussion group. The real value of the study is in the discussion questions. We all see life differently and the thoughts and ideas shared in a group will often lead to a richer understanding of the Scripture. The questions often require the participant to put himself (herself) in the mind or circumstances of that person in the Scriptures.

The commentary portion of the introductory material in each lesson is there to help clarify the passage and set the stage for the discussion questions. The questions are designed to help the student understand the meaning of the text itself and explore the kingdom implications from a personal point of view.

Ideal For Both New and Mature Bible Students

These lessons have three underlying questions:

- "Who is this person?"
- "What is happening here?"
- "What is the implication for my life?"

Because of the obscurity of the characters under study, chances are that even experienced participants with prior understanding of the lesson's theme will find fresh material to explore. Both new and long-time students will be challenged by the life lessons these unfamiliar characters can teach them.

Format of Lessons

Each lesson begins with the Scripture using the ESV translation followed by short sections titled "Context," "What Do We Know," and "Observations." The discussion questions are designed to help the student understand the subject and are followed by several application questions.

Blasphemy

Grace

Quarrels

&

Reconciliation

Paralytic Man
lowered through roof

**Occurrences of "paralytic" and "four men"
in the Bible:** 5/1

Themes: Faith; Forgiveness; Blasphemy

Scripture

Mark 2:1-12
And when he returned to Capernaum after some days, it was reported that he was at home. 2 And many were gathered together, so that there was no more room, not even at the door. And he was preaching the word to them. 3 And they came, bringing to him a paralytic carried by four men. 4 And when they could not get near him because of the crowd, they removed the roof above him, and when they had made an opening, they let down the bed on which the paralytic lay. 5 And when Jesus saw their faith, he said to the paralytic, "My son, your sins are forgiven." 6 Now some of the scribes were sitting there, questioning in their hearts, 7 "Why does this man speak like that? He is blaspheming! Who can forgive sins but God alone?" 8 And immediately Jesus, perceiving in his spirit that they thus questioned within themselves, said to them, "Why do you question these things in your hearts? 9 Which is easier, to say to the paralytic, 'Your sins are forgiven,' or to say, 'Rise, take up your bed and walk'? 10 But that you may know that the Son of Man has authority on earth to forgive sins"—he said to the paralytic — 11 "I say to you, rise, pick up your bed, and go home." 12 And he rose and immediately picked up his bed and went out before them all, so that they were all amazed and glorified God, saying, "We never saw anything like this!" ESV

This story also appears in Matthew 9:2-8 and Luke 5:17-26.

1

The Context

In the first chapter of Mark, the author had already described several miraculous healings. Jesus' popularity was such that large crowds were beginning to gather wherever He went. Some just wanted to hear what He had to say, but many were seeking healing of some kind. So when the paralytic arrived at the house there were people everywhere and no way to carry him into the house. The text says they could not even get past the door.

Beginning with this account of the paralytic, Mark relates various stories, ending with Mk 3:6, all of which result in challenging Jesus about His authority, actions, or teaching. This first story results in Jesus being accused of blasphemy because He forgave the sin of the paralytic. The Jews knew that the ability and power to forgive rebellion against God resided only with the Divine, so in claiming to forgive, Jesus was claiming to be equal to God – *blasphemy*!

What Do We Know?

Either the four men had great faith and determination or the paralytic's health was so bad that they were driven by friendship or compassion to get him before Jesus. The four men carrying the paralytic were so determined that even the large crowds at the house did not deter them. Why they chose the roof option is not known or obvious, but they made it work.

The process of digging through the roof is not described. We don't know what help they might have had from inside or outside on the roof. The text simply reports they made a hole and lowered the paralytic to Jesus. Frankly, that is all we really need to know! The actual process has no spiritual implications.

Following the healing the paralytic "immediately" got up and walked. Everyone saw him, including the scribes. There is no report of atrophy or time needed to walk. There is no question about how the paralytic was healed: Jesus spoke life into his body . . . and he was healed.

Observations

It must have been very interesting to have been in the house when the four men began digging the hole in the roof. One could logically assume they dug above the room in which Jesus was speaking, but it is possible they came down in an adjoining room. This would not have been a clean and tidy operation. Dirt and branches would have been falling over an extended period of time and space – it would not have been easy to get a hole in the roof large enough to lower a man. Can you imagine Jesus stopping His speaking, watching and waiting for the operation to reach its conclusion? It is certainly possible that Jesus knew what was going on and kept the crowd in check while the hole was being dug.

The people in the room would not have known why somebody was digging through the roof. If this was Peter's home (speculation based on 1:21, 29) and he was present and could see what was happening, he might not have been happy. In fact, we can imagine that he might have tried to make his way to the roof to stop the destruction of his home.

We never hear about the paralytic again in the Bible. Why? Do you think he just disappeared into the background? Did he have a short or long life? How long did the excitement of his healing last? Did he eventually become a disciple of Jesus? Was he ever a strong proponent of the Gospel, witnessing to others about what Jesus did for him? Was he obnoxious and did he drive people away from the Gospel? What was the paralytic's legacy?

The question of the paralytic's legacy can be inspiring or it might be disappointing. We do not really know. But the message for us is not really the paralytic. The message for us is Jesus. What did He do and how does that impact our lives? Is it time to dig a hole?

Discussion Questions

<u>A. GENERAL:</u>

A1. Verse 2 says that Jesus was preaching the Word to the crowd. What do you think that means? He certainly wasn't preaching the resurrection yet!

A2. What reasons (other than great faith or paralytic's very poor health) can you think of for the dedicated determination or faith of these four men?

A3. What other access options were available to the four men other than digging a hole in roof?

A4. How difficult do you think it was to dig through the roof?

A5. Do you think anyone in the room below helped?

A6. What would have happened in today's society if something like this took place?

A7. What is Jesus saying about Himself when He tells the paralytic that his sins are forgiven?

A8. In 2:5 Mark says that Jesus saw "their" faith. Whose faith is He talking about? Faith in what? What kind of faith did Jesus see?

A9. Since the paralytic is obviously coming to be physically healed, why do you think the first thing that Jesus says is that the paralytic's sins are forgiven?

A10. If the scribes had believed that Jesus was the Messiah, would forgiving sins have been acceptable?

A11. In 2:7 the scribes said that only God could forgive sins. Does this make sense? If I am the one sinned against, can't I forgive the one who sinned against me?

A12. What do you think Jesus means in 2:9 when He asked which was easier, forgiving sins or healing a paralytic?

For God: _____

For man: _____

A13. Why does Jesus heal the paralytic?

A14. How did Jesus normally respond when the crowds asked Him to perform a sign?

A15. Why were the scribes there? [Hint: look back to 1:21-22]

A16. The people in attendance were amazed (astonished). Have you ever been truly amazed at something? What was it and how did you feel or how were you impacted? Have you ever witnessed a miracle?

A17. The Matthew version of this story says that Jesus told the paralytic to go home after he picked up his mat. Why would Jesus tell the man to go home? Is that what you would have done if you had just been healed?

A18. The Shema, a Jewish confession of faith, begins with reference to Dt 6:4 that says, "*Hear, O Israel: The Lord our God, the Lord is one!*" This confession stresses the unity and singleness of God: there are not multiple Gods. Jesus quoted from the Shema in Mark 12:28-30. How would an understanding and knowledge of this confession make it easy for most Jews to reject the idea that Jesus was the Son of God or that the Messiah was the Son of God?

B. Blasphemy

B1. What is the basis for the scribes' claim that Jesus was blaspheming? [Hint: see John 10:33]

B2. Based on Mark 14:64, why was Jesus crucified?

B3. What is blasphemy?

B4. Is the reasoning of the scribes in Mark 2:7 wrong?

C. APPLICATION

C1. Have you ever been so needy or desirous of something that you took extraordinary measures to accomplish your goal? How about today? Do you need to boldly persevere in something?

C2. Is your faith equal to that of the four bearers? If not, why not? How strong is your faith?

C3. Would you have dug a hole in the roof when you arrived at the house? Why or why not?

C4. What would make your faith stronger?

C5. Do you need to <u>dig a hole</u> for someone?

Joseph of Arimathea
who buried Jesus

**Occurrences of "Joseph of Arimathea"
in the Bible:** 1-2 in each Gospel

Themes: A disciple

Scripture – the burial of Jesus

Mark 15:42-46
And when evening had come, since it was the day of Preparation, that is, the day before the Sabbath, 43 Joseph of Arimathea, a respected member of the Council, who was also himself looking for the kingdom of God, took courage and went to Pilate and asked for the body of Jesus. 44 Pilate was surprised to hear that he should have already died. And summoning the centurion, he asked him whether he was already dead. 45 And when he learned from the centurion that he was dead, he granted the corpse to Joseph. 46 And Joseph bought a linen shroud, and taking him down, wrapped him in the linen shroud and laid him in a tomb that had been cut out of the rock. And he rolled a stone against the entrance of the tomb. ESV

John 19:38-42
After these things Joseph of Arimathea, who was a disciple of Jesus, but secretly for fear of the Jews, asked Pilate that he might take away the body of Jesus, and Pilate gave him permission. So he came and took away his body. 39 Nicodemus also, who earlier had come to Jesus by night, came bringing a mixture of myrrh and aloes, about seventy-five pounds in weight. 40 So they took the

body of Jesus and bound it in linen cloths with the spices, as is the burial custom of the Jews. 41 Now in the place where he was crucified there was a garden, and in the garden a new tomb in which no one had yet been laid. 42 So because of the Jewish day of Preparation, since the tomb was close at hand, they laid Jesus there. ESV

Additional Information in Matthew and Luke:
Matthew 27:57, *60*
. . . a rich man from Arimathea, named Joseph, who also was a disciple of Jesus. . . . . 60 and laid it in his own new tomb, which he had cut in the rock. And he rolled a great stone to the entrance of the tomb and went away ESV

Luke 23:50-51
Now there was a man named Joseph, from the Jewish town of Arimathea. He was a member of the council, a good and righteous man, 51 who had not consented to their decision and action . . . ESV

The Context

This burial story appears in all four Gospel accounts. Jerusalem was crowded because of the Passover Festival, and the crucifixion of Jesus was the main topic of conversation.

Mark reports that Jesus let out a loud cry and breathed His last. The followers of Jesus who were in attendance on that day would have heard Him say, "It is finished." Mark also tells us that it was late in the evening on Preparation day – the day before the Sabbath (a Friday).

The soldiers had come to break the legs of the three hanging on the crosses in order to hasten their death so that the bodies would not hang on the crosses during the Sabbath. They did not break Jesus' legs because they observed He was already dead. But just to be sure, one of the soldiers pierced His side with a spear, causing water and blood to spill from His body.

What Do We Know?

This study is primarily about Joseph of Arimathea, not about the burial of Jesus. However, Joseph is mentioned only in connection with the death and burial of Christ. Let's note what the following tells us about Joseph:

Mk 15:43   He was a <u>respected member</u> of the Sanhedrin.

Mk 15:43   He was <u>looking for</u> the kingdom of God.

Mk 15:43   He took <u>courage</u> and went to Pilate and asked for the body of Jesus.

Jn 19:38   He was a <u>disciple</u> of Jesus.

Jn 19:38   He was acting in <u>secret</u>.

Lk 23:50   He was described as a <u>good and righteous</u> man.

Lk 23:51   He had <u>not</u> consented to the Sanhedrin's plans and actions regarding Jesus.

The Kingdom of God

Mark 15:43 says that Joseph of Arimathea was looking forward to *the kingdom of God*, and John reports Jesus as saying, "*My kingdom is not of this world,*" or in other words, our kingdom does not have its origin here. (John 18:36)

John 18:36 confirms that Jesus has a kingdom, but He says it is <u>not</u> of this world, probably meaning it is not the kind of kingdom the Jews were expecting. His kingdom will not be a military kingdom, or a kingdom on earth where Jesus, the Messiah, would rule by force. The kingdom that Jesus ushered into being would not include the traditional triumphal victory parade desired by the Jewish population. This kingdom arrived inconspicuously in a manger and

13

was tiny like a mustard seed or like a pearl of great value. The people were expecting a time when God would directly rule over His people. Joseph was looking forward to the rule of God and may have believed that Jesus was the one who would rule.

When the Scripture says that Joseph was looking ahead to the kingdom we don't know for sure what he is thinking. We do know that Jesus was preaching about the kingdom (Mt 9:35) and when asked about it by John the Baptist, He replied as follows:

> Matt 11:2-5   *Now when John heard in prison about the deeds of the Christ, he sent word by his disciples 3 and said to him, "Are you the one who is to come, or shall we look for another?" 4 And Jesus answered them, "Go and tell John what you hear and see: 5 the blind receive their sight and the lame walk, lepers are cleansed and the deaf hear, and the dead are raised up, and the poor have good news preached to them." ESV*

Jesus' description of what He was doing was consistent with the prophecies in Isaiah 29:18, 35:4-6, and 61:1, so both John the Baptist and Joseph of Arimathea should have concluded that Jesus was the Messiah:

> Isa 61:1   *The Spirit of the Lord God is upon me, because the Lord has anointed me to bring good news to the poor; he has sent me to bind up the brokenhearted, to proclaim liberty to the captives, and the opening of the prison to those who are bound. ESV*

Discussion Questions

A. GENERAL

A1. At this moment (the death of Jesus), what do you think the Jesus-followers, including Joseph, were thinking? What would have been your state of mind at that time?

A2. If the above is true, why would Joseph give the tomb and take the body, etc.?

A3. What would normally have been done with the bodies of criminals who had been crucified?

A4. What do you think Joseph risked by asking for the body?

A5. Do you think this identified Joseph as a disciple of Jesus?

A6. Why would Joseph take such a risk for a dead body?

A7. What might have happened to Joseph once Pilate and the Sanhedrin knew that Joseph wanted the body of Jesus to bury in his tomb?

PILATE

SANHEDRIN

A8. Do you think there is any significance to this being a new and unused tomb?

A9. How can you explain Jesus' quick death?

A10. Why do you think Pilate gave the body to Joseph?

A11. Normally the family claimed the body. Why do you think Mary and her family did not do that?

A12. How does the fact that Joseph went "boldly" (took courage) to Pilate compare with Joseph's attitude prior to Jesus' death?

A13. Put yourself in Joseph's sandals. You have kept your faith quiet, possibly for many months. Do you think Joseph may have felt guilty for never speaking up about Jesus to the Jewish leaders?

A14. What impact do you think it would have had if either or both Joseph and Nicodemus had spoken up in front of the Sanhedrin?

A15. What do you think changed for Joseph that he would come forward now? Explain.

A16. Mark 14:64 and Luke 23:1 tell us that all of the Sanhedrin condemned Jesus and that He deserved death. Yet in Luke 23:51 it says that Joseph did not agree with the Sanhedrin's plans. How do you explain what seems to be a contradiction?

B. BEING A DISCIPLE

B1. Both John and Matthew tell us that Joseph of Arimathea was a disciple. What do you think it means that Joseph was a disciple of Jesus? How would you define "disciple"?

B2. John reports three times how Jesus described a disciple. What do these verses tell us about being a disciple of Jesus?

John 8:31   _____

John 13:35   _____

John 15:8   _____

B3. If Joseph was truly a disciple of Christ Jesus, then how does he conscientiously serve as a member of the Sanhedrin?

B4. What conflicts of interest would occur while Joseph remained a secret disciple of Jesus?

B5. Why do you think Joseph kept his belief in Jesus secret?

B6. Can you be saved and not be a disciple?

C. APPLICATION

C1. Are you a disciple of Jesus? Is there enough evidence to convict you? Do you *obey*, *love*, and produce *fruit*?

C2. Do you have any conflicts of interest with Christ and His teachings? For example do you disagree with or <u>not</u> believe some key portion of His teaching? How do you harmonize your position?

C3. Do you belong to any secular organization that inherently rejects some of the teachings of Christ or puts loyalty to the organization above all else?

C4. Do you know anyone who "played a part" or did not reveal true feelings, opinions or position about Christ (like Joseph and Nicodemus)? How did things work out?

C5. Mark 15:42 says that Joseph was looking forward to the kingdom of God. Are you? Why? Why not?

Joanna & Susanna

benefactors

**Occurrences of "Joanna" and "Susanna"
in the Bible:** 2/1

Themes: Benefactors; Support

Scripture

Luke 8:1-3   Many Women Support Christ's Work
*Soon afterward he went on through cities and villages, proclaiming
and bringing the good news of the kingdom of God. And the twelve
were with him, 2 and also some women who had been healed of
evil spirits and infirmities: Mary, called Magdalene, from whom
seven demons had gone out, 3 and Joanna, the wife of Chuza,
Herod's household manager, and Susanna, and many others, who
provided for them out of their means.*   ESV

Luke 24:9-11
*and returning from the tomb they told all these things to the eleven
and to all the rest. 10 Now it was Mary Magdalene and Joanna and
Mary the mother of James and the other women with them who
told these things to the apostles, 11 but these words seemed to
them an idle tale, and they did not believe them.* ESV

References to "women" that may have included Joanna or
Susanna:

Matt 27:54-56
*When the centurion and those who were with him, keeping
watch over Jesus, saw the earthquake and what took place,
they were filled with awe and said, "Truly this was the Son*

*of God!" 55 There were also many women there, looking on
from a distance, who had followed Jesus from Galilee,
ministering to him, 56 among whom were Mary Magdalene
and Mary the mother of James and Joseph and the mother
of the sons of Zebedee.* ESV [also Mk 15:40-41]

Luke 23:26-31
*And as they led him away, they seized one Simon of Cyrene,
who was coming in from the country, and laid on him the
cross, to carry it behind Jesus. 27 And there followed him a
great multitude of the people and of women who were
mourning and lamenting for him. 28 But turning to them
Jesus said, "Daughters of Jerusalem, do not weep for me,
but weep for yourselves and for your children. 29 For
behold, the days are coming when they will say, 'Blessed
are the barren and the wombs that never bore and the
breasts that never nursed!' 30 Then they will begin to say
to the mountains, 'Fall on us,' and to the hills, 'Cover us.' 31
For if they do these things when the wood is green, what
will happen when it is dry?"* ESV

The Context

The identification of Joanna and Susanna as benefactors and
supporters of Christ occurs at the beginning of Luke, chapter 8. The
only other reference to Joanna is as one of the women who went
to the tomb on resurrection morning. No further information is
given about Joanna, except that she and her companions reported
what they saw and heard at the tomb. Joanna and the other
women (Mary Magdalene, Mary the mother of James and some
others) were told of Jesus' resurrection from the dead by two
angelic beings. These women went back and gave the eleven
disciples the news of Jesus' resurrection. (Luke 24:10).

The passage in Luke 8 occurred as Jesus was traveling, preaching,
and teaching in Galilee with the twelve Apostles. He was also
traveling with some women, three of whom are named: Mary
Magdalene, Susanna, and Joanna. Joanna was identified as the wife

of Chuza who was Herod's steward. The text then says in referring to these three and many others [presumably other women] that they "were supporting them from their possessions." The NIV says that they were "supporting them out of their own means."

What Do We Know?

Joanna, Susanna, and possibly other women and men, were supporting Jesus' ministry and His twelve disciples out of their own wealth or income. The money would have been used to buy and arrange for meals, shelter, and other necessities. We know that Scripture reports Jesus staying in homes at various times, but it is likely He spent many nights sleeping outside under the stars when homes were not available. When this occurred, meals would have been cooked over open fires for all those traveling with Jesus.

We don't know the actual number of people traveling or how often they were able to find a place for their mats in the homes of supporters. The women would have had to be prepared for whatever circumstances were presented to them. It is likely that on some nights a few were able to eat and sleep in a home or shelter while the remaining travelers were forced to eat and sleep outside.

Since nothing is ever said about Jesus or His Apostles carrying supplies, bags, or mats, it is probably a reasonable assumption that all this was being handled by the women. If there were twenty men in the traveling band plus the women support staff, there was probably a significant amount of "stuff" to be transported from place to place – perhaps even requiring carts.

Observations

The first thing to recognize is that whatever the women were doing for the traveling band, it was acceptable to Jesus. If what they were doing was inappropriate or unnecessary or over-taxing, Jesus could have altered the responsibilities of the women or disbanded them altogether. It is likely that the women made the work of the ministry a little more tolerable. The ministry that Jesus and the disciples were doing would have been both physically and emotional draining. Not having to worry about meals, shelter, setting up camp, and all the other travel necessities would have been very appealing to the men involved in the ministry.

The Bible describes Jesus's work of ministry, but never speaks of Him and His disciples collapsed from exhaustion at the end of the day. We really don't have much of a view of them trying to escape the crowds that were pursuing them. We get a hint on several occasions, but I suspect these reports don't give us the whole picture of how the traveling band was really living.

Another interesting phenomenon is the diversity of the support staff. The fact that Joanna was married to one of King Herod's officials suggests that she was well-to-do. She probably had substantial means and in fact may have been supplying a major portion of the money required to support the traveling band. In addition, the difference in social or cultural status between Joanna and the other women, some of whom had questionable or sinful backgrounds, would certainly have been interesting. The fact that no difficulties are reported is a credit to these women.

Discussion Questions

A. GENERAL

A1. Do you think Jesus chose the people who traveled with Him?

A2. What problem might have occurred if Jesus chose the women who could follow? What might have happened if He had told someone she could not be in the group?

A3. Do you think that this arrangement of the women following and supporting Jesus and the disciples would have been looked on with favor?

> 1) By friends of men with wives or daughters in the traveling band:

> 2) By society in general:

> 3) By Pharisees:

A4. If you were a women's rights activist, how would you use theses passages about women to support your activist position?

> FAVOR:

> DISFAVOR:

A5. What conclusions can you draw from the difference in what we know of Mary Magdalene and Joanna and their status or backgrounds?

A6. List the things the "many women" might have done for Jesus and the other disciples.

A7. How important would you say Joanna and Susanna were to Jesus and the disciples?

A8. We know that Joanna was married to Chuza. How do you suppose she was able to leave home and her husband and travel around Galilee?

A9. Do you suspect that the other women were unmarried?
Married? Why? If they were unmarried, what was the source of
their income to support Jesus and His Apostles?

A10. How would society have looked on either married or
unmarried women traveling around with Jesus?

A11. What might Chuza's friends and enemies have said about this
situation with his wife?

A12. Where do you suppose all these people were sleeping when
they were traveling around? There could easily have been 20+
people in the support group.

A13. Could there have been more than one group?

A14. What is the possibility that husbands of these women (or sons and brothers) were also part of the traveling group?

A15. Why do you suppose these women did all this work and gave their money? What could have been the motivation?

A16. Do you suppose this band of women became a closed group? Why? Why not?

A17. Do you think these women would have stayed with the traveling band or would they have gone home when they got tired?

A18. Do you think one of the women emerged as the leader? If so, who in the group of women might have been the leader, and why?

A19. Would the Apostles have allowed a woman to hold the money if a "treasurer" was necessary?

.

A20. Comparing the timelines of Luke 8 and 24, we learn that the women stayed the course. They did not leave after a couple of months and were there to the bitter end. What might you conclude from the fact that the women did not leave but stayed to prepare His body after the crucifixion?

A21. How do you suppose these women felt as they stood at a distance from the cross?

A22. Why do you think they stood at a distance?

B. APPLICATION

B1a. Women: Would you have been one of the women if you had had the opportunity? Why? Why not?

B1b. Men: If you were married and either your spouse or daughter wanted to join this traveling group, would you have permitted it:

      1) if living in Jesus day.

      2) today.

B2. How would you compare your own commitment to Jesus to this traveling band?

B3. Do you know anyone who is obviously sold out to Jesus and would have followed Jesus around the countryside or joined His support group?

      Q. What is different about them?

B4. If you had witnessed the cross, how would you have felt? Would you have understood? Would you have watched?

Ananias
messenger to Saul (Paul)

Occurrences of "Ananias" in the Bible: 6

Themes: Grace; Sovereignty; Power

Note: The name "Ananias" occurs eleven times in Scripture, six times in reference to the messenger God used in Damascus. It occurs twice in reference to a High Priest and three other times in reference to the couple (Ananias and Sapphira) in Acts 5 who lied about the proceeds of the land they sold.

Scripture

Acts 9:10-20

Now there was a disciple at Damascus named Ananias. The Lord said to him in a vision, "Ananias." And he said, "Here I am, Lord." 11 And the Lord said to him, "Rise and go to the street called Straight, and at the house of Judas look for a man of Tarsus named Saul, for behold, he is praying, 12 and he has seen in a vision a man named Ananias come in and lay his hands on him so that he might regain his sight." 13 But Ananias answered, "Lord, I have heard from many about this man, how much evil he has done to your saints at Jerusalem. 14 And here he has authority from the chief priests to bind all who call on your name." 15 But the Lord said to him, "Go, for he is a chosen instrument of mine to carry my name before the Gentiles and kings and the children of Israel. 16 For I will show him how much he must suffer for the sake of my name." 17 So Ananias departed and entered the house. And laying his hands on him he said, "Brother Saul, the Lord Jesus who appeared to you on the road by which you came has sent me so that you may regain your sight and be filled with the Holy Spirit." 18 And immediately something like scales fell from his eyes, and he regained his sight. Then he rose and was baptized; 19 and taking food, he was strengthened. For some days he was with the disciples at Damascus. ESV

<u>Acts 22:12-16   Paul Telling the Story</u>
And one Ananias, a devout man according to the law, well-spoken of by all the Jews who lived there, 13 came to me, and standing by me said to me, 'Brother Saul, receive your sight.' And at that very hour I received my sight and saw him. 14 And he said, 'The God of our fathers appointed you to know his will, to see the Righteous One and to hear a voice from his mouth; 15 for you will be a witness for him to everyone of what you have seen and heard. 16 And now why do you wait? Rise and be baptized and wash away your sins, calling on his name.' ESV

The Context

We find the story of Ananias in Acts 9:10 where Luke (the author) tells about Ananias and his participation in Saul's conversion and baptism. Saul will soon be known as Paul but that name change has not yet occurred. Saul had been on his way to Damascus to arrest any Christians he could find. He had permission from the High Priest to go to the synagogues in Damascus, arrest anyone associated with "The Way," and bring them back to Jerusalem. Damascus probably had the biggest Jewish community outside of Israel. It was about 150 miles from Jerusalem – a 4-7 day walk.

While Saul was still near Damascus on the road, he was confronted by the living Christ. A light from heaven rendered him helpless. He fell to the ground and heard Jesus speaking to him. Jesus told Saul to go into the city where he would be told what to do by a man named Ananias.

When Saul got up from the ground he was blind. He had to be led into Damascus by his friends. The text says that Paul did not eat or drink anything for three days. The scene in the story then shifted from Paul's encounter on the road to Jesus telling Ananias to be the messenger who would give Saul his instructions.

What Do We Know?

Ananias was a disciple in Damascus and the Lord appeared or spoke to him in a vision. He recognized the voice or appearance in the vision and Jesus gave Ananias the following instructions:

- Go to the house of Judas on Straight Street.
- Ask for Saul.
- Place your hands on Saul (meaning to pray).

The result would be that Saul's sight was restored. Understandably Ananias was afraid, concerned, and unsure and he told Jesus in the vision that Saul was an "enemy" who came to Damascus to arrest Christian under the authority of the chief priest. Jesus knew all this, of course, and did not react to Ananias' concern but told him that He had special plans for Saul. Jesus even revealed some of these plans to Ananias.

That was apparently good enough for Ananias because he immediately did exactly what Jesus asked him to do. Ananias went to the house, placed his hands on Saul, asked that "Brother Saul" see again, and that he be filled with the Holy Spirit. The text reports that something "like scales" fell from Saul's eyes and he was able to see again. He got up and was baptized by one of the disciples.

Observations

Straight Street in Damascus still exists today. It's a large straight street that travels east and west through the city, in contrast to the winding streets throughout other parts of the city. It would have been easy for Ananias to find Judas' house. Since Ananias lived in Damascus it would have taken little time to get to the designated house to meet with Saul. We don't know exactly how long it took Saul to arrive at the house from where he was blinded, but we know that he was blind for three days before Ananias arrived (9.9).

We have some hints about what Paul experienced prior to Ananias' arrival. We know that he was blind and had to be led around by hand. Jesus told Ananias that Saul was praying. And 9:12 says that

Saul had a vision in which a man named Ananias came and restored his sight. Saul may have been praying for Ananias to show up so that he could see again. Or, he might have been praying for forgiveness. The text tells us nothing about Saul's prayer.

We only can speculate about what Saul was going through. He would have come to understand that what he had been doing was wrong, that he had not correctly understood the Scriptures, and that he had been part of the crowd that murdered Jesus, the Son of God. We know that Saul understood Jesus to be the Son because that is what he began preaching in the synagogues immediately after he regained his strength from the blindness and fasting (9:20).

We do not know how and when Ananias had become a committed Jesus-follower. He might have been in Jerusalem at Pentecost and heard and saw all that took place. He might have been in the crowds listening to one of Peter's sermons. In any case he had become a believer and was living in Damascus. He may have been one of the Christians that Saul would have rounded up had he not been blinded on the road.

Summary

This story demonstrates several of God's attributes:

Grace: Saul was called into the Kingdom although he had persecuted the church. He did not deserve this favor.

Patience: Jesus did not punish Saul for his behavior until he was on the way to Damascus. He also gave him a three-day delay to live with his blindness.

Power: In a light from heaven Jesus spoke directly to Saul. He also gave Saul both blindness and healing.

Forgiveness: Jesus forgave Saul for persecuting followers of The Way (9:5). He also called Saul to ministry.

Mercy: He did not punish Saul for his merciless treatment of believers. He healed Saul's blindness.

Sovereignty: Jesus spared Saul and chose him to be the apostle to the Gentiles.

Love: Jesus healed Saul and caused Ananias to accept Saul as a brother and pray for him.

Discussion Questions

A. GENERAL

A1. What do we learn about Ananias in 9:10 and 22:12?

      a) He was a _____ of Christ.

      b) He was a _____ man.

      c) He had a _____ reputation among the local Jews.

NOTE: This is all we know about Ananias, other than the things that happened to him in this story and how he responded.

A2. What does it mean that Ananias was "devout"?

A3. What do you think it means that he was devout, <u>according to the Law</u>?

A4. We see both similarities and differences in Jesus' encounters with Saul and with Ananias:

> Similarities:
> (a) Both heard Jesus' voice.
> (b) Both received instructions from Jesus.
> (c) Both obeyed Jesus.
> Differences:
> (a) Saul saw a light but Ananias did not.
> (b) Saul didn't recognize Jesus' voice; Ananias did.
> (c) Saul was blinded but Ananias suffered no physical infirmity.

What can we learn about Ananias in observing what he did and said in these following two passages?

Acts 9
(1) He responded to the Lord _____ .

(2) He recognized Jesus' voice and responded, _____

_____ .

(3) He questioned Jesus: Are you sure? This is the man who had been _____ everyone.

(4) He went to the house where Saul was staying, entered, and addressed Saul as _____ .

(5) He _____ _____ on Saul.

(6) He told Saul that Jesus had sent him, so that:

        a) he might _____ again, and

        b) he might be filled with the _____ _____ .

Acts 22:

(7) Ananias came, stood by Paul and said "_____ Saul, regain your sight."

(8) Then he said:
> Acts 22:14-15   *And he said, "The God of our fathers appointed you to know his will, to see the Righteous One and to hear a voice from his mouth; 15 for you will be a witness for him to everyone of what you have seen and heard."*   ESV

(9) Ananias told Saul to get up and be baptized and wash away his
_____.

A5. Why do you think God explained His plans for Saul to Ananias?

A6. How would you have felt going to the house to confront Saul? Would you have called him brother?

A7. What is the significance of Ananias calling him "Brother"?

A8. The accounts of what Ananias said to Saul are very different in Acts 9:17 and Acts 22:14-15. Luke does not report that Ananias said any of the things that Paul described in Acts 22! In Acts 9:15-16 Luke reports that Jesus told Ananias that Saul was His chosen instrument, to take Gospel message to Gentiles, kings, and the Israelites, and he would suffer much in this service.

Why do you think the information reported about Jesus' plans for Saul in Acts 9 was so different from that in Acts 22?

A9. Did Saul fulfill Jesus' plans as outlined in Acts 22:14-15?

A10. Jesus told Ananias His special plans for Saul in Acts 9:

      (a) He was God's chosen instrument.

      (b) He would carry His name before the Gentiles, their kings, and the people of Israel.

      (c) He would suffer for the name of Jesus.

Do you think Ananias understood any of this at the time?

A11. Why did God choose Ananias for this assignment? Why didn't God heal and restore Saul without the use of a third party?

A12. How would Saul have been received by believers in Damascus if God had not used Ananias?

A13. Why was Jesus not unhappy with Ananias voicing his concerns about going to Saul? Wasn't Ananias questioning God's plans and instructions?

A14. How did God respond to Ananias' concerns about meeting with an enemy of the church?

A15. Who did Ananias say appeared to Saul and what are the implications?

A16. Based on 9:20 how do we know that Saul got the message?

A17. Do you think Saul's physical condition had any impact on him when Ananias arrived to pray for him?

A18. Verse 9:11 says that Saul was praying. If you had been Saul, what would you have been praying?

A19. Jesus chose Ananias for this job because Ananias was devout and Jesus knew he would do as He asked. This was an important task and would have considerably elevated Ananias' standing among his friends in the Christian community. Yet, we never hear about Ananias again. Why?

A20. How are the following attributes of God demonstrated in this story?

Grace: _____

Patience: _____

Power: _____

Forgiveness: _____

Mercy: _____

Sovereignty: _____

Love: _____

B. APPLICATION

B1. Do you know anyone who needs an Ananias in his or her life?

.

B2. Do you know an Ananias?

B3. Have <u>you</u> ever been an Ananias to someone?

B4. Is there anyone in your life who needs grace?

B5. What part of Saul's experience has happened in your life?

- Prior to conversion persecuting believers.
- Prior to conversion aggressively rebelling against God.
- Dramatic encounter with Jesus (a Damascus Road experience).
- Spent days in fasting and prayer before dramatic revelation.
- Eyes opened to the truth by another believer.

Hymenaeus
shipwrecked faith

Occurrences of "Hymenaeus" in the Bible: 2

Themes: Opposition; Blasphemy; Stand Firm

Scripture

<u>1 Tim 1:18-20</u>   Christ Jesus Came to Save Sinners
This charge I entrust to you, Timothy, my child, in accordance with the prophecies previously made about you, that by them you may wage the good warfare, 19 holding faith and a good conscience. By rejecting this, some have made shipwreck of their faith, 20 among whom are Hymenaeus and Alexander, whom I have handed over to Satan that they may learn not to blaspheme. ESV

<u>2 Tim 2:14-26</u>   A Worker Approved by God
Remind them of these things, and charge them before God not to quarrel about words, which does no good, but only ruins the hearers. 15 Do your best to present yourself to God as one approved, a worker who has no need to be ashamed, rightly handling the word of truth. 16 But avoid irreverent babble, for it will lead people into more and more ungodliness, 17 and their talk will spread like gangrene. Among them are Hymenaeus and Philetus, 18 who have swerved from the truth, saying that the resurrection has already happened. They are upsetting the faith of some. 19 But God's firm foundation stands, bearing this seal: "The

*Lord knows those who are his," and, "Let everyone who names the
name of the Lord depart from iniquity."*

*20 Now in a great house there are not only vessels of gold and
silver but also of wood and clay, some for honorable use, some for
dishonorable. 21 Therefore, if anyone cleanses himself from what is
dishonorable, he will be a vessel for honorable use, set apart as
holy, useful to the master of the house, ready for every good work.*

*22 So flee youthful passions and pursue righteousness, faith, love,
and peace, along with those who call on the Lord from a pure heart.
23 Have nothing to do with foolish, ignorant controversies; you
know that they breed quarrels. 24 And the Lord's servant must not
be quarrelsome but kind to everyone, able to teach, patiently
enduring evil, 25 correcting his opponents with gentleness. God
may perhaps grant them repentance leading to a knowledge of the
truth, 26 and they may escape from the snare of the devil, after
being captured by him to do his will.* ESV

The Context

Timothy was one of the Apostle Paul's young co-workers. Paul
wrote two letters to Timothy instructing him about leadership and
how to live out his faith in the Christian community in Ephesus. It
was very important to Paul that the right doctrine be taught and
communicated to the church. But it was equally important that
Timothy live out that doctrine for all to see. Paul wanted Timothy
to confront false teaching and he warned him about the kind of
problems and opposition he would be likely to face.

In 1 Tim 1:3-4 Paul warned Timothy specifically about false
teachers:

> 1 Timothy 1:3-4
> *As I urged you when I was going to Macedonia, remain at
> Ephesus that you may charge certain persons not to teach*

*any different doctrine, 4 nor to devote themselves to myths
and endless genealogies, which promote speculations
rather than the stewardship from God that is by faith.* ESV

Later in that same chapter Paul identified several people who were
creating problems. One of them was Hymenaeus, who was
mentioned only briefly in this first letter but then to a greater
extent in Paul's second letter to Timothy. Paul was very concerned
about doctrine and encouraged Timothy to stand firm:

2 Tim 1:14   *By the Holy Spirit who dwells within us, guard
the good deposit entrusted to you.* ESV

2 Tim 3:14   *But as for you, continue in what you have
learned and have firmly believed, knowing from whom you
learned it.* ESV

2 Tim 4:2 . . . *preach the word; be ready in season and out
of season; reprove, rebuke, and exhort, with complete
patience and teaching.* ESV

What Do We Know?

In the 1 Timothy passage Paul said he expected Timothy would face
a spiritual battle. Paul warned Timothy that some followers had
rejected the truth, resulting in their faith being "shipwrecked."
Paul said he had handed Hymenaeus over to Satan in order to be
taught not to blaspheme. The text does not explain what this
"handing over" means.

In the 2 Timothy passage, Paul gave several warnings, admonitions,
and instructions about Christian living. Paul was doing two things:
(1) giving Timothy instruction and reminders, and (2) listing issues
and warnings relative to Hymenaeus. Some of his suggestions were
to:

2:14   Stop quarreling over words ("word-smithing");
        it is of little value to anyone.

2:15   Correctly handle or <u>teach</u> the Word of God.

2:16   Avoid godless chatter – it leads to ungodly
        behavior.

2:22a   Flee from the evil desires of youth.

2:22b   Pursue righteousness, faith, love, and peace.

2:22c   Seek the Lord with a pure heart.

2:23   Avoid foolish arguments because they produce
        quarrels.

2:24   Avoid quarrels; be kind to everyone.

2:25   Gently instruct those who oppose you.

In 2:18-19 Paul says that Hymenaeus had wandered away or deviated from the truth. Paul says that Hymenaeus and Philetus claimed that the resurrection had already taken place, probably implying that there is no bodily resurrection. Others believed this heresy and were led astray.

Paul pointed out that the world contains both good and bad people, and both good and bad activities, but God will use the man who cleanses himself from unrighteousness. Quarreling and arguing about words will not be useful. In 2:23-24 Paul warned Timothy again about quarreling, which he had previously mentioned in 2:14 (Holman translates it "fight about words"). An example of this type of quarreling would be an argument about whether the "days" in the Genesis creation story are 24-hour days, seasons, or ages consisting of many years.

Paul's final advice to Timothy was to instruct the heretics gently. Timothy might have felt like taking drastic action, but Paul said he must allow God to do His transforming work.

Observations

2 Tim 2:15   *Do your best to present yourself to God as one approved, a worker who has no need to be ashamed, rightly handling the word of truth.* ESV

This one verse tells us a great deal about what Paul desired for Timothy. Regardless of what was going on around him and regardless of the impact Hymenaeus had on other believers, Timothy should first and foremost look after his own life situation. Paul gave him the following advice:

- Do your best.
- Present yourself approved of God.
- Be at work.
- Do not be ashamed.
- Correctly "handle" the word of truth.

Doing your "best" might also be translated as "be zealous," which gives this admonition a feeling of eagerness or strong commitment that will not waver. Paul wanted Timothy to have a passionate desire for God's approval. He and we should not rest or quit until we have achieved the goal of God's approval. Paul's powerful statement that he is not ashamed of the Gospel rings throughout the New Testament:

> Rom 1:16   *For I am not ashamed of the gospel, for it is the power of God for salvation to everyone who believes, to the Jew first and also to the Greek.* ESV

> 2 Tim 1:12   *which is why I suffer as I do. But I am not ashamed, for I know whom I have believed, and I am convinced that he is able to guard until that Day what has been entrusted to me.* ESV

Timothy would achieve all this by making sure he taught the Word of God correctly, accurately, unashamedly, as a co-worker with Paul, and ultimately for Christ. Timothy would not sugarcoat the Gospel to make everybody happy. It is the very truth and the power of God.

Discussion Questions

A. GENERAL

A1. What does Paul mean by the word "shipwrecked" in 1 Tim 1:19?

A2. What should you do if you have something on your conscience concerning the work you are trying to do?

A3. Do you think Paul did everything required by Mt 18:15-17?
Matt 18:15-17   *If your brother sins against you, go and tell him his fault, between you and him alone. If he listens to you, you have gained your brother. 16 But if he does not listen, take one or two others along with you, that every charge may be established by the evidence of two or three witnesses. 17 If he refuses to listen to them, tell it to the church. And if he refuses to listen even to the church, let him be to you as a Gentile and a tax collector. ESV*

A4. What does it mean when Paul says he handed Hymenaeus over to Satan?
NOTE: 1 Cor 5:5 *you are to deliver this man to Satan for the destruction of the flesh, so that his spirit may be saved in the day of the Lord.* ESV

A5. What do you think Paul means in 2 Tim 2:18 that Hymenaeus has "swerved from the truth"?

A6. Who else is to blame if someone "wanders" away from the truth?

A7. The "What Do We Know?" section above lists nine suggestions from 2:14 – 2:25. What do the first three and the last three have in common, and how important is that common theme?
[see James 3:5-12]

A8. What do we learn in James 3:6-10 about the "tongue"?

James 3:6-10   *And the tongue is a fire, a world of unrighteousness. The tongue is set among our members, staining the whole body, setting on fire the entire course of life, and set on fire by hell. 7 For every kind of beast and bird, of reptile and sea creature, can be tamed and has been tamed by mankind, 8 but no human being can tame the tongue. It is a restless evil, full of deadly poison. 9 With it we bless our Lord and Father, and with it we curse people who are made in the likeness of God. 10 From the same mouth come blessing and cursing. My brothers, these things ought not to be so.* ESV

Q. Do you think it is really true that man, on his own cannot tame the tongue?

Q. Do you think your tongue can set the course of your life? What important or critical life decision can you make without using your tongue?

Q. What do you think is the worst characteristic of the tongue?

B. BLASPHEME

B1. What does it mean for someone to blaspheme (1 Tim 1:20)?

B2. Can you imagine today if we had a law like this today? How would secular people react?

B3. How would Hymenaeus be taught not to blaspheme by "handing him over to Satan"?

B4. How does the Scripture Paul quoted in 2 Tim 2:19 support his argument?

2 Tim 2:19   *But God's firm foundation stands, bearing this seal: "The Lord knows those who are his," and, "Let everyone who names the name of the Lord depart from iniquity."* ESV

B5. Paul says in 2 Tim 2:21 that if a person is right with God he can be used, and then he lists four specific ways. What are they and what do they mean?

2 Tim 2:21   *Therefore, if anyone cleanses himself from what is dishonorable, he will be a vessel for honorable use, set apart as holy, useful to the master of the house, ready for every good work.* ESV.

B6. In 2:22 Paul lists five more instructions. What are they and what is the significance of the phrase "*along with those who call on the Lord from a pure heart*"?

C. ARMOR OF GOD

C1. Paul lays much of the blame for Hymenaeus' falling away on Satan. How does Paul tell us to fight with Satan in Ephesians 6?

C2. When you are fighting evil, who or what are you fighting based on Eph 6:10ff?

D. ARGUMENTS

D1. In 2:24 why would Paul imply that if Timothy engaged in "quarrels" he would not be able to teach?

D2. Have you ever won an argument? Who wins an argument?

E. RESURRECTION

E1. If what Hymenaeus is promoting is an early form of Gnosticism, then he does not believe in the <u>bodily</u> resurrection. How does Paul confront this error in 1 Cor 15? Paul examined the claim that there was no bodily resurrection and draws a number of conclusions about this false belief.

> 1 Corinthians 15:12-19
> *Now if Christ is proclaimed as raised from the dead, how can some of you say that there is no resurrection of the dead? 13 But if there is no resurrection of the dead, then not even Christ has been raised. 14 And if Christ has not been raised, then our preaching is in vain and your faith is in vain. 15 We are even found to be misrepresenting God, because we testified about God that he raised Christ, whom he did not raise if it is true that the dead are not raised. 16 For if the dead are not raised, not even Christ has been raised. 17 And if Christ has not been raised, your faith is futile and you are still in your sins. 18 Then those also who have fallen asleep in Christ have perished. 19 If in this life only we have hoped in Christ, we are of all people most to be pitied. ESV*

Q. What are the problems or issues if Jesus has not been resurrected?

1. Christ has not been _____

2. Our preaching is without _____

3. Our faith is without _____

4. We are false witnesses about _____

5. Our faith is _____

6. We are still in our _____

7. Those who have previously died have also _____

8. We should be pitied.

E2. What difference does it make whether or not you believe in the bodily resurrection?

E3. What significant doctrine of the Gospel can you argue is true if you do not believe in the resurrection?

F. APPLICATION

F1. Do you believe in the bodily resurrection? Why? Can you support your belief?

F2. Do you like to argue over the meaning or interpretation of little things? Do you focus on insignificant details and fail to see the bigger picture?

> FOR EXAMPLE:
> (a) Do you need to know when the rapture is going to occur in the tribulation period?

> (b) Do you need to know whether creation occurred in 6 days or 6 ages?

> (c) Do these things matter to you?

F3. Do you have any concerns about the truth of any part of Scripture? Is there anything whose truth you doubt?

F4. If you were Timothy, what would you personally think are the two most important and relevant things Paul has told <u>you</u> in this passage?

F5. Do you know anyone like Hymenaeus?

G. EXERCISE

Choose <u>one</u> of the six admonitions in 2 Tim 2:15 (see next page) and explain what that particular admonition means in light of all that Paul is telling Timothy.

2 Tim 2:15   *Do your best to present yourself to God as one approved, a worker who has no need to be ashamed, rightly handling the word of truth.* ESV

1) do your best (be diligent)
2) present yourself
3) as one approved of God
4) a worker
5) not be ashamed
6) rightly handling the word of truth

_____

_____

_____

_____

_____

_____

_____

_____

_____

_____

_____

_____

_____

_____

_____

_____

_____

_____

_____

_____

_____

_____

_____

_____

_____

_____

_____

_____

_____

_____

_____

_____

_____

_____

_____

Euodia & Syntyche
Paul's co-workers

**Occurrences of "Euodia" and "Syntyche"
in the Bible:** 1/1

Themes: Quarrels; Reconciliation; Unity

Scripture

Philippians 4:2-7   Exhortation, Encouragement, and Prayer
I entreat Euodia and I entreat Syntyche to agree in the Lord. 3 Yes, I ask you also, true companion, help these women, who have labored side by side with me in the gospel together with Clement and the rest of my fellow workers, whose names are in the book of life.

4 Rejoice in the Lord always; again I will say, Rejoice. 5 Let your reasonableness be known to everyone. The Lord is at hand; 6 do not be anxious about anything, but in everything by prayer and supplication with thanksgiving let your requests be made known to God. 7 And the peace of God, which surpasses all understanding, will guard your hearts and your minds in Christ Jesus. ESV

> EUODIA: [you OH dih uh] (good journey) [3] (Nelson's)

> SYNTYCHE: [SIN tih keh] (fortunate) [4] (Nelson's)

The Context

The Bible's only reference to Euodia and Syntyche occurs in this one location at the end of Paul's letter to the Philippians. It is not an afterthought (the subject of the admonition is important), but the disunity that exists between the women is <u>probably</u> not of the earth-shaking variety. Something's created a division between these two co-workers and Paul pauses to insert this mild admonition, hoping that it would help resolve whatever had come between these two women.

What Do We Know?

We do not know the details of the problem that created the rift between the two women. We can reasonably assume that the issue is not a moral failure or some theological concern, because if it were, Paul would certainly have addressed the problem more thoroughly. All Paul does is call attention to the disunity and "entreat" the women to agree. Paul then asked a companion to help the women resolve their differences.

We don't know a great deal about the two women but it seems likely they were active in ministry with Paul. They were apparently not part of a "work" group that arranged for sleeping quarters and food because Paul says that they "*contended for the gospel at my side.*" This would imply they were in a more direct active ministry with Paul. There is no way to determine if these two women were in leadership positions of some kind, but it is certainly possible.

Observations

Our western society has created many divisions and separations that produce walls, antagonism, and competition in our daily lives. These differences promote disharmony, disunity, and suspicion, which often lead to quarreling, anger, and even physical confrontation. Can you add any to the following list?

Nation vs Nation	School vs School	Good vs Bad
White vs Blue Collar	State vs State	Union vs Non-union
Right vs Wrong	Employer vs Employee	City vs City
Liberal vs Conservative	Healthy vs Sick	Business vs Business
City vs Rural	Class vs Class	Rich vs Poor
Church vs Church	Government vs Citizens	Male vs Female
Lawful vs Lawless	Old vs Young	Team vs Team

_____

_____

_____

_____

There may be more drama behind this situation that we are not told. Paul does not reveal what is causing the disagreement between the two women but it is obvious that he is not taking sides. He simply urges them to "agree in the Lord."

Discussion Questions

A. GENERAL

A1. What does "entreat" mean in 4:2?

A2. What do you think Paul is trying to convey by using the same instruction to both women?

A3. Paul asks the women to "agree in the Lord." What do you think that means?

A4. Why do you think Paul is not more specific?

A5. Do you think Paul is asking the women to absolutely agree? Why? Why not?

A6. If Paul is not saying they must come to an absolute agreement, then what is he saying?

A7. What do you think this disagreement is all about? How might you characterize it?

A8. Why would Paul bring up this issue between these two women? Why would he care if a couple of members disagreed about something, particularly when the difference does not appear to be a major problem?

A9. Paul makes a unique comment about the people these women helped. What is it and what does it mean?

A10. Why would Paul mention the faith status of Clement and the co-workers? Why do you think Paul found it necessary to say their names were in the book of life?

A11. Paul is writing this letter to the Philippians while he is in prison in Rome. How might Paul know about this disagreement between the two women? Obviously a visitor may have told him, or he may have received a letter or note from someone in the congregation. What can we reasonably conclude about the disagreement from the fact that Paul knows about it?

B. QUARRELING

Quarreling can mean different things to different people. Generally it implies that some person, thing, idea, or concept is the basis for a disagreement or conflict that could become an argument or altercation.

B1. What words or phrases might you use to describe a quarrel?

B2. What are the possible results or outcomes of a quarrel?

B3. Since Paul does not mention any moral failure or theological issue we can reasonably assume that this may be a petty disagreement. If that is true, how might this situation impact the local church at Philippi?

C. RESOLUTION

I think it is possible that Php 4:4-7 and maybe 4:8 are a direct continuation of Paul's concern about the conflict between Euodia and Syntyche. Most commentaries do not relate these two passages but a closer look at what they are saying reveals answers to the question of how to resolve situations like this which have created some level of disharmony in the church. With that purpose in mind, what are Paul's suggestions on resolution? How do each of the following fit into the scenario that they are suggestions for resolving the conflict between the two women?

C1. _____

4 Rejoice in the Lord always; again I will say, Rejoice. ESV

C2. _____

5a Let your reasonableness be known to everyone. ESV

C3. _____

5b The Lord is at hand; ESV

C4. _____

6 do not be anxious about anything, but in everything by prayer and supplication with thanksgiving let your requests be made known to God. ESV

C5. _____

7 And the peace of God, which surpasses all understanding, will guard your hearts and your minds in Christ Jesus. ESV

C6. _____

8 Finally, brothers, whatever is true, whatever is honorable, whatever is just, whatever is pure, whatever is lovely, whatever is commendable, if there is any excellence, if there is anything worthy of praise, think about these things. ESV

D. UNITY

A quarrel or dispute can begin as a minor annoyance but escalate to an all-out war if it is allowed to fester. It might get so bad that it impacts the unity of the church. This may be the reason that Paul mentions this situation. Jesus was also concerned about unity. In John 17 Jesus prayed for Himself, His then present disciples, and last for the believers who would come after them. This prayer comes just before Jesus goes to the cross and the most important issue on His mind, relative to the church, is unity (John 17:20-26).

D1. How would you describe or define Christian unity?

D2. How did Jesus define unity in John 17:20-23?

John 17:21-23   *21 that they may all be one, just as you, Father, are in me, and I in you, that they also may be in us, so that the world may believe that you have sent me. 22 The glory that you have given me I have given to them, that they may be one even as we are one, 23 I in them and you in me, that they may become perfectly one, so that the world may know that you sent me and loved them even as you loved me. ESV*

D3. Based on Eph 4:3-6 how might you argue that unity is a foundational tenet of the Christian faith?

Eph 4:3-6   *eager to maintain the unity of the Spirit in the bond of peace. 4 There is one body and one Spirit—just as you were called to the one hope that belongs to your call— 5 one Lord, one faith, one baptism.* ESV

For <u>one</u> of the following seven characteristics, enter a description on how it relates to unity:

one body: _____

one Spirit: _____

one hope: _____

one Lord: _____

one faith: _____

one baptism: _____

one God: _____

D4. What inherent aspects of unity make it a desirable trait within the church?

D5. The purpose of unity is identified throughout Scripture. For example, we find the following:

Jn 17: 21, 23   So the world will know.

Ro 15:5-6   So God is glorified.

Eph 4:13   So we become mature.

Jn 12:44-45   So others see and believe.

Ps 133 (ESV)   When Brothers Dwell in Unity
Behold, how good and pleasant it is when brothers dwell in unity!
2 It is like the precious oil on the head, running down on the beard,
on the beard of Aaron, running down on the collar of his robes! 3 It
is like the dew of Hermon, which falls on the mountains of Zion!
For there the Lord has commanded the blessing, life forevermore.

What is the purpose of unity identified in Ps 133 above?

D6. Based on Eph 4:2, how are we to achieve unity?

Ephesians 4:2-3   *with all humility and gentleness, with patience, bearing with one another in love, 3 eager to maintain the unity of the Spirit in the bond of peace.* ESV

E. APPLICATION

E1. In your opinion how important is Christian unity?

E2. Are you prone to quarreling?

E3. What one thing might be said or remembered about you? [Note: Euodia and Syntyche's names appear nowhere else in Scripture. They are remembered for just one thing: they were quarreling and creating disharmony in the church.

What about you?

E4. Is it your nature to be argumentative or a peacemaker? Ephesians 4:3 says we are to be eager to maintain unity. Does that describe you, your friends, your church . . . ?

E5. Is there a situation in your life that needs *agape* reconciliation?

Elimelech, Mahlon & Chilion
they all died

Occurrences of "death" "die" "dead" or "died"
in the Bible: 1252

Themes: Physical Death

NOTE: The above number of occurrences means that <u>on average</u> in a normal Bible without study notes, one of these words appears on nearly every page.

Scripture

Ruth 1:3-5   Naomi's Family
But Elimelech, the husband of Naomi, died, and she was left with her two sons. 4 These took Moabite wives; the name of the one was Orpah and the name of the other Ruth. They lived there about ten years, 5 and both Mahlon and Chilion died, so that the woman was left without her two sons and her husband. ESV

The Context

Elimelech and his two sons Mahlon and Chilion are each mentioned 3-4 times in the Bible. The only reason they are mentioned is so the author can identify their family and report that they died.

Unless you are alive when Jesus returns for His church you will experience the death of your physical body. There are many ways to experience death – naturally from old age, because of illness, as a result of war, from an accident or murder, or even suicide. The Scriptures above relate to several deaths as they are reported in the Bible. Romans 6:23 reminds us of the underlying reason for death – sin! But in the same verse Paul tells us the good news of the Gospel – life!

Most believers think of God as the God of life but in reality that is not a complete picture. Our God is the God of both life and death:

> Deuteronomy 32:39   *See now that I, even I, am he, and there is no god beside me; I kill and I make alive; I wound and I heal; and there is none that can deliver out of my hand.* ESV

If our God were not the God of death, we might be in a sad state of affairs. We have a righteous God over both life and death. We can be assured of His justice in dealing with sin, which is the root cause of death:

> Rom 6:16, 21   *Do you not know that if you present yourselves to anyone as obedient slaves, you are slaves of the one whom you obey, either of sin, which leads to death, or of obedience, which leads to righteousness? . . . 21 But what fruit were you getting at that time from the things of which you are now ashamed? The end of those things is death.* ESV

> James 1:15   *Then desire when it has conceived gives birth to sin, and sin when it is fully grown brings forth death.* ESV

What Do We Know?

The one thing we can state with certainty is this: We are going to die! We have all heard the saying "the only sure things in this world are death and taxes." The death part of that saying is confirmed in Psalm 89:47-48:

> Psalms 89:47-48   *Remember how short my time is! For what vanity you have created all the children of man! 48 What man can live and never see death? Who can deliver his soul from the power of Sheol?* ESV

Some may argue with the statement, "everyone will die" because of two Biblical examples. The Bible implies that Enoch (Gen 5:24) and Elijah (2 Kings 2) didn't die. However, if they happen to be the Two Witnesses (Rev 11:3), then there is still the possibility that everyone prior to the Second Coming will experience physical death.

Death of the body is a subject many do not want to discuss, or even think about. Christians with a saving faith in Christ will have eternal life with an immortal resurrected body, but for this short study we're considering only death of the physical body.

Given the certainty of physical death, it's ironic that we do so little to understand it or prepare for its coming. Responsible people write wills and prepare end-of-life directives, but many don't even do that. It's almost a mind-set of "If I don't think about it, it won't happen," or "I'll think about that when I'm old and nearly ready to die." But death doesn't wait until we're ready for it.

Some people are so caught up with the desire to be remembered in this world that they do unnecessary and worthless things. They chase a dream of some sort of immortality, not realizing that real life begins only after death. Scripture reminds us that we will quickly be forgotten – like a puff of smoke.

> Ecclesiastes 1:10-11   *Is there a thing of which it is said, "See, this is new"? It has been already in the ages before us. 11 There is no remembrance of former things, nor will there be any remembrance of later things yet to be among those who come after.* ESV [see also Eccl 2:16, 9:5-6]

> Ps 62:9   *Those of low estate are but a breath; those of high estate are a delusion; in the balances they go up; they are together lighter than a breath.* ESV [Also James 4:14]

In the grand scheme of things you and I are not very important. Yet, the God of the universe has numbered the hairs on our heads! Explain that if you can!

Man's life today is lived out under a sentence of death. God's original creation did not include death, but that is the current reality since Adam sinned, and it will remain that way until Jesus returns. We should be more aware of this ultimate destiny because we could die at anytime and anywhere. It is such an intimidating subject to so many that we "put it on the back burner" and then ignore the entire reality of death.

One cannot reasonably think about or consider death without understanding the reason that death permeates the human race: sin! Paul, in his letter to the Romans, tells us what we need to know:

> Romans 5:12   *Therefore, just as sin came into the world through one man, and death through sin, and so death spread to all men because all sinned.* ESV

Sin is the reason that death entered Creation and until that problem is ultimately eliminated, man must deal with the woes of death.

Discussion Questions

A. GENERAL

A1. If sin is the real cause of death, then how should we think about sin?

A2. What are some things about death that people worry about?

A3. What can you conclude about death by considering those who died with Saul (1 Sam 31:6)?
1 Samuel 31:6 *Thus Saul died, and his three sons, and his armor-bearer, and all his men, on the same day together.* ESV
HINT: Compare the deaths of Saul and his sons to that of the armor-bearer.

A4. Is the death of a believer any different than that of an unbeliever? If so, what is the difference?

(1) the actual death: _____

(2) the circumstances leading up to the death:_____

_____

(3) the funeral:_____

A5. Has the impact of death on people's lives in Biblical times and now changed much?

A6. Do you think Ps 39:4 is a good prayer? Why? Why not?
Ps 39:4   *O Lord, make me know my end and what is the measure of my days; let me know how fleeting I am!*   ESV

A7. Are <u>you</u> fearful of death? Do you know anyone who is? How can you overcome this fear or help someone else overcome it?

A8. Do you think death is a fair, just, or reasonable sentence for sinful behavior? Why? Why not?

A9. How would you argue that the fear of death is:

Good:

Bad:

A10. What does Heb 2:14-15 bring into the discussion and what does it mean?

Heb 2:14-15   *Since therefore the children share in flesh and blood, he himself likewise partook of the same things, that through death he might destroy the one who has the power of death, that is, the devil, 15 and deliver all those who through fear of death were subject to lifelong slavery.* ESV

A11. How does the devil hold the power of death?

A12. Psalms 90:12 says, *"So teach us to number our days that we may get a heart of wisdom."* ESV

(1) What does this mean in general?

(2) What does it mean to <u>you</u> personally?

A13. How might a "bucket list" be good or bad for someone in the latter portion of their life?

<u>Good:</u>

<u>Bad:</u>

A14. How is death both the weakest and strongest element in God's salvation plan?

Weakest:

Strongest:

A15. If Jesus paid the penalty for our sin, then why must we die?

A16. 1 Corinthians 15:19 says, "*If in this life only we have hoped in Christ, we are of all people most to be pitied.*" What do you think this means?

B. FEAR OF DEATH

B1. What does Heb 2:15 say that we are freed from?
Hebrews 2:15 *and deliver all those who through fear of death were subject to lifelong slavery.* ESV

B2. How could you overcome your fear of death?

    <u>Unbeliever:</u>

    <u>Believer:</u>

C. UTOPIA

C1. A major understanding or belief in secular culture is that dying opens the way to a higher state of consciousness where we live a better life. Why would people believe this view?

C2. How is this view in conflict with Christian belief?

C3. If a nonbeliever says, "death is nothing at all, all is well, I can handle death" how would you respond?

D. APPLICATION

D1. Are you being honest with God about <u>your</u> fears of death?
       [or with family, friends . . .]

D2. What concerns you most about getting old? Is it something you can do anything about?

D3. What worries <u>you</u> most about dying?

D4. Do you think that leaving a legacy is important? Why? How could you leave a legacy that honors God?

D5. What would you <u>personally do</u> if you knew you were going to die 3 months from now?

D6. What might <u>your</u> greatest and least priorities be in D5 above?

Greatest: _____

_____

Least: _____

_____

Cornelius

a centurion

Occurrences of "Cornelius" in the Bible: 8

Themes: Gentiles; Jewish customs

Note: There are at least five different centurions identified in the Bible:
*Acts 10:	Cornelius, the Gentile convert.
*Acts 21, 22, 23, 24:	Arrested Paul in Jerusalem.
	At Paul's flogging.
	Paul tells he is Roman citizen.
*Acts 27:	Julius(2)/Centurion(5)Takes Paul to Rome.
*Lk 23:47; Mt 27 and Mk 15:	Centurion at the cross.
*Mt 8 and Luke 7:	Faith of centurion heals his servant.

Scripture

Acts 10:1-31

At Caesarea there was a man named Cornelius, a centurion of what was known as the Italian Cohort, 2 a devout man who feared God with all his household, gave alms generously to the people, and prayed continually to God. 3 About the ninth hour of the day he saw clearly in a vision an angel of God come in and say to him, "Cornelius." 4 And he stared at him in terror and said, "What is it, Lord?" And he said to him, "Your prayers and your alms have ascended as a memorial before God. 5 And now send men to Joppa and bring one Simon who is called Peter. 6 He is lodging with one Simon, a tanner, whose house is by the seaside." 7 When the angel who spoke to him had departed, he called two of his servants and a devout soldier from among those who attended him, 8 and having related everything to them, he sent them to Joppa.

9 The next day, as they were on their journey and approaching the city, Peter went up on the housetop about the sixth hour to pray. 10 And he became hungry and wanted something to eat, but while they were preparing it, he fell into a trance 11 and saw the heavens opened and something like a great sheet descending, being let down by its four corners upon the earth. 12 In it were all kinds of animals and reptiles and birds of the air. 13 And there came a voice to him: "Rise, Peter; kill and eat." 14 But Peter said, "By no means, Lord; for I have never eaten anything that is common or unclean." 15 And the voice came to him again a second time, "What God has made clean, do not call common." 16 This happened three times, and the thing was taken up at once to heaven.

17 Now while Peter was inwardly perplexed as to what the vision that he had seen might mean, behold, the men who were sent by Cornelius, having made inquiry for Simon's house, stood at the gate 18 and called out to ask whether Simon who was called Peter was lodging there. 19 And while Peter was pondering the vision, the Spirit said to him, "Behold, three men are looking for you. 20 Rise and go down and accompany them without hesitation, for I have sent them." 21 And Peter went down to the men and said, "I am the one you are looking for. What is the reason for your coming?" 22 And they said, "Cornelius, a centurion, an upright and God-fearing man, who is well spoken of by the whole Jewish nation, was directed by a holy angel to send for you to come to his house and to hear what you have to say." 23 So he invited them in to be his guests.

The next day he rose and went away with them, and some of the brothers from Joppa accompanied him. 24 And on the following day they entered Caesarea. Cornelius was expecting them and had called together his relatives and close friends. 25 When Peter entered, Cornelius met him and fell down at his feet and worshiped him. 26 But Peter lifted him up, saying, "Stand up; I too am a man." 27 And as he talked with him, he went in and found many persons gathered. 28 And he said to them, "You yourselves know how unlawful it is for a Jew to associate with or to visit anyone of another nation, but God has shown me that I should not call any person common or unclean. 29 So when I was sent for, I came without objection. I ask then why you sent for me." 30 And

*Cornelius said, "Four days ago, about this hour, I was praying in my
house at the ninth hour, and behold, a man stood before me in
bright clothing 31 and said, 'Cornelius, your prayer has been heard
and your alms have been remembered before God. ESV*

The Context

This event takes place in the early days of the church after the
resurrection. Philip had met the Ethiopian official on the road to
Gaza, Saul (Paul) had experienced his conversion on the road to
Damascus, and Peter was preaching to large crowds and had
recently healed the paralytic Aeneas in Lydda and raised Tabitha
(Dorcas) from the dead in Joppa.

From Joppa Peter was called to Caesarea, a town about 30 miles
north of Joppa. Caesarea was the headquarters for the Roman
soldiers that occupied Israel. There Peter met with a centurion
named Cornelius who, although a Gentile, was described as being
devout and God-fearing. A centurion normally commanded a
military group that consisted of at least 100 men.

Summary

Cornelius had a vision in which he saw an angel of God. The angel
told him to send men to Joppa and bring Peter to Caesarea to meet
with Cornelius. At about the same time Peter, in Joppa, fell into a
trance and saw a strange scene of unclean animals and was told to
"kill and eat." Peter initially refused, saying he would not break the
dietary laws. The voice in the vision told him not to call anything
impure that God had made clean. This scene recurred three times
and then the vision ended and Peter awakened.

As Peter thought about what he had just seen, the men sent by
Cornelius arrived at the gate and asked to speak with Peter. The
Holy Spirit directed Peter to go with the men to meet with

Cornelius. Peter invited the men into his house and the next day left with them for Caesarea. Peter arrived at Cornelius' home where a large crowd of friends and relatives had gathered. Peter said that although it was against Jewish law for him to enter the home of a Gentile, God had shown him that the barriers between the Jew and the Gentile had been removed.

Cornelius told Peter of his vision and said he and his family were gathered there to hear what God had commanded Peter to tell them. Peter said that he now understood that God would accept anyone who feared Him (Jew or Gentile) and proclaimed the Gospel of Christ to them.

While Peter spoke, the Spirit of God fell on the Gentiles just as it had previously on Jewish believers. This was confirmed as the Gentiles began speaking in other languages and praising God – presumably similar to what had happened on the Day of Pentecost. Peter then ordered the Gentiles to be baptized and he stayed on at the home of Cornelius.

Observations

It is clear that in this early stage of the church that the Jewish Christians did not know or understand the Gospel was available to all who would accept Jesus as Lord and Savior. But with this event, God made it clear that the Jews did not have an exclusive relationship with Him. Entrance into the Kingdom of God would now be made available to anyone – both Jew and Gentile. This, of course, was a difficult change for many Jews! Two thousand years of culture and history had taught them that they were the chosen people. Being descendant of Abraham and circumcision were the only requirements to be in good standing with God.

A major shift in God's salvation plan had been introduced to these Jewish believers and it would take some time and effort for that change to work itself into the fabric of religious life. Ultimately most Jews would reject this new understanding and stubbornly maintain that Jesus was not their Messiah and not the Son of God.

Therefore when Peter went to Jerusalem (11:2) the circumcised believers there criticized him for associating with Gentiles. Peter did not defend his actions but explained what had happened, particularly his vision of the unclean animals and God's direction to "kill and eat." Peter reported that upon hearing the Gospel, Cornelius and his household received the Holy Spirit just as the Jews had on Pentecost. As a result:

Acts 11:18   *When they heard these things they fell silent. And they glorified God, saying, "Then to the Gentiles also God has granted repentance that leads to life."* ESV

Discussion Questions

A. GENERAL

A1. What was a centurion?

A2. How are Cornelius and his family described?

A3. What would it mean today to say someone is "devout"?

A4. What did it mean that Cornelius was "God-fearing"?

A5. Why wasn't what Cornelius did (devotion, God-fearing, etc.) enough for Paul?

A6. What makes someone a Gentile?

A7. What does 10:4 confirm?

Acts 10:4 . . . *"What is it Lord?" And he said to him, "Your prayers and your alms have ascended as a memorial before God."* ESV

A8. Cornelius was told to send for Peter who was staying with a tanner in Joppa. What is significant about this?

A9. What happened to Peter on the roof and how does it differ from what happened to Cornelius?

    <u>Peter:</u>

    <u>Cornelius:</u>

A10. What is significant about the animals in Peter's vision?

A11. How did these dietary laws impact the relationships between Jews and Gentiles?

A12. God gave Peter the vision three times. Why didn't He just directly communicate the acceptance of the Gentiles in some form that was absolutely clear? Why the vision of the animals, etc.?

A13. How would you explain what God told Peter in 10:15?

Acts 10:15   *And the voice came to him again a second time, "What God has made clean, do not call common."* ESV

A14. How did Peter come to the understanding in 10:28 that the wall between Jew and Gentile had been removed?

A15. What could Peter point to as evidence that all this was true?

A16. What did Peter say he had learned in 10:34-35?

A17. In your opinion what is the most important statement in Peter's sermon?

A18. Find at least one other passage in Scripture that says salvation is available to all who believe in Jesus.

A19. How did Peter and the Jews traveling with him know that Cornelius and his household should be baptized?

A20. Peter did not get angry or defensive. How did he respond? (11:4)

A21. What exactly are the truths God was communicating in this event?

B. APPLICATION

B1. There were barriers that had to be overcome to allow Gentiles to come into the church. Are there barriers of any kind in your life or in your church that need to be broken down or removed? Who in your community would think that your church is not for them?

B2. Who do you consider "unclean" or unfit to be in church? Who are you putting outside the grace and mercy of God?

B3. What would you do if a Muslim started attending your church?

B4. Cornelius was already devout and a God-fearer, but he still needed Jesus. This is because everyone needs Jesus. Nobody is worthy, nobody is without sin, and someone or something <u>must</u> remove the sin debt. Do you understand that there is a sin debt? Do you think there is anyone other than Jesus who can remove or pay the sin debt?

Now What?

Get Wisdom – General Information:

www.getwisdompublishing.com

Get Wisdom – Resources:

You can access free resources from Get Wisdom by going to:

www.getwisdom.link/resources

Grace and the Gravel Road:

Grace & the Gravel Road teaches both the Truth+Tools that Christ-followers need to fully live the life God has for them.

www.graceandthegravelroad.com

You Can Help:

Mention The *OBSCURE* Bible Study Series on your social platforms. Include the hashtag #obscureBiblestudy so we are aware of your post.

Recommend *OBSCURE* to your family, friends, small group, Sunday School class leaders, or your church.

Thanks so much!

The *OBSCURE* Bible Study Series

Meet Shamgar, Jethro, Manoah & Hathach
An introduction to the OBSCURE Bible Study Series.

This book of four lessons is provided at a reduced cost so that students and leaders can get a first-hand experience and introduction to The *OBSCURE* Bible Study Series.

Blasphemy, Grace, Quarrels & Reconciliation
The intriguing lives of first-century disciples.

This book presents Joseph of Arimathea, Joanna, Ananias, Hymenaeus, and Cornelius (a centurion). It illustrates the nature and challenges of life as a first-century disciple. Life has real challenges, but they can be overcome.

The Beginning and the End
From creation to eternity.

This book has four lessons from Genesis and four from the book of Revelation. It covers such topics as creation, rebellion, grace, worship, and eternity. It illustrates how God is leading us to worship in the Throne Room.

God at the Center
He is sovereign and I am not.

This book examines the virgin birth, worship, prayer, the sovereignty of God, compromise, and trust. God is at the center of all these stories. He is there in the shadows or openly orchestrating our lives. Regardless of the situation He is at the center of our lives – a sovereign almighty God.

Women of Courage
God did some serious business with these women.

This book examines the lives of Jael, Rizpah, the woman of Tekoa, Tabitha, Shiphrah, and Lydia. We see these women exhibiting great courage and faithfulness. God used them in amazing ways and we can use their example for encouragement and spiritual leadership.

The Beginning of Wisdom
Your personal character counts.

In this book we find courage, loyalty, thankfulness, love, forgiveness, and humility. Personal character counts. It is critical to make good decisions because they have consequences. Building our lives on wisdom will help us stand firm in our faith. We should reject the example of Demas who deserted Paul for the values of the world.

Miracles & Rebellion
The good, the bad, and the indifferent.

This book contrasts characters who rebelled against God with those who trusted in Him. God hates sin and loves to heal the faithful. The rebellion of Korah, Haman, and Alexander are included to compare with the healing stories of Aeneas, a slave girl, and the crippled man at Lystra.

The Chosen People
There is a remnant.

This book concentrates mostly on Israel in the Old Testament, but also covers some interesting subjects as Lucifer, Michael the archangel, and Job's wife.

The Chosen Person
Keep your eyes on Jesus.

The focus of this book is on Jesus and the superiority of Christ. We investigate Melchizedek, the disciples on the road to Emmaus, Nicodemus, the criminal on the cross who asks to be remembered by Jesus, and others.

Acknowledgments

Arlene
Arlene has served as wife, editor, and proof-reader for all of my writing – thank you for your patience, help, and love.

Michelle
Michelle, our older daughter, has been an invaluable resource. She was the first author in the family: graceandthegravelroad.com.

Stephanie
Our middle daughter designed all the covers for the *OBSCURE* Bible Study Series, as well as the marks and logos for Get Wisdom Publishing. We are grateful for her talent!

KOINONIA Small Group
These dear friends have hung in there with me as I taught many of the lessons to them first. Their input, answers, and suggestions on many of the lessons has been invaluable.

God, Jesus, and Holy Spirit
Thank you, Lord, for Your guidance and direction.

Notes

1. Nelson's Illustrated Bible Dictionary, Copyright © 1986, Thomas Nelson Publishers; from PC Study Bible, "Euodia"

2. Nelson's Illustrated Bible Dictionary, Copyright © 1986, Thomas Nelson Publishers; from PC Study Bible, "Syntyche"

About the Author

Steve attended church as a child and accepted Christ when he was 10 years old. But his walk with Jesus left a lot to be desired for the next 44 years. In 1994 he "wrestled" with God for some period of months and in September of that year totally surrendered his life to Jesus.

In 1996 he was so driven to study God's Word that he attended the Indianapolis campus of Trinity Evangelical Divinity School (Chicago) to earn a Certificate of Biblical Studies. His hunger for God's Word led him to lead and write all his own Bible studies for his small group. He has been an entrepreneur and Bible study leader for the past 25 years.

In 2019 he was one of four members who founded The Acanthus Group (www.theacanthusgroup.org). He is a member of The Church at Station Hill in Spring Hill, TN, a regional campus of Brentwood Baptist (Brentwood TN).

www.getwisdompublishing.com

Key Points To Remember

Record ideas, thoughts, and concepts you want to remember.

_____

_____

_____

_____

_____

_____

_____

_____

_____

_____

_____

_____

_____

_____

_____

_____

_____

_____

_____

_____

_____

_____

_____

_____

_____

_____

_____

_____

_____

_____

_____

_____

_____

_____

_____

_____

_____

_____

_____

_____

_____

_____

_____

_____

_____

_____